Tigers

NorthWord Press

Minnetonka, Minnesota

With special thanks to the staff of the Tiger Information Center
–G.S.

Photography © 2002: Erwin & Peggy Bauer: p. 40; Adam Jones/Danita Delimont, Agent: p. 16; Claudia Adams/Dembinsky Photo Associates: back cover, p. 31; Terry Whittaker/Dembinsky Photo Associates: p. 41; D. Robert & Lorri Franz: p. 6; Alan & Sandy Carey: pp. 15, 20-21, 27, 28-29, 32-33, 34, 42-43; Brian Kenney: pp. 4, 8-9, 10; Tom & Pat Leeson: cover, pp. 11, 17, 24; Anup Shah: pp. 5, 18, 22, 37, 38-39, 44; Art Wolfe: pp. 12-13.

Illustrations by John F. McGee
Designed by Russell S. Kuepper
Edited by Aimee Jackson

NorthWord Press
5900 Green Oak Dr
Minnetonka, MN 55343
1-800-328-3895
www.northwordpress.com

Library of Congress Cataloging-in-Publication Data

Swain, Gwenyth
    Tigers / Gwenyth Swain ; illustrations by John F. McGee.
        p. cm. -- (Our wild world series)
    Summary: Describes the physical characteristics, behavior, and habitat of tigers.
    ISBN 1-55971-808-0 (hc.) -- ISBN 1-55971-797-1 (soft cover)
    1. Tigers--Juvenile literature. [1. Tigers.] I. McGee, John, ill. II. Title. III. Series.

QL737.C23 S87 2002
599.756--dc21   2001054619

Printed in Singapore

10 9 8 7 6 5 4 3 2 1

Tigers

Gwenyth Swain
Illustrations by John F. McGee

NORTHWORD PRESS
Minnetonka, Minnesota

WITH THEIR LARGE JAWS, powerful legs, and broad paws, tigers are really big! Male tigers can weigh over 670 pounds (300 kilograms). But with all their size, these great hunters move with the silence and grace of their relative the house cat. Tigers are one of 37 species (SPEE-sees), or kinds, of cats living on our planet today. Of all the different species of wild cats, tigers are the largest.

The tiger's scientific name is *Panthera tigris*. There are eight different groups, or subspecies (sub-SPEE-sees), of tigers. Over time, these different groups of tigers developed in different ways, depending on where they lived. Three subspecies of tiger are now extinct, or no longer living. They once prowled the islands of Java and Bali in Indonesia and the shores of the Caspian Sea in Asia.

Today, five subspecies of tigers roam areas of Asia from eastern Russia in the north to the island of Sumatra in the south. They are the Siberian (or Amur) tiger, the Sumatran tiger, the Indo-Chinese tiger, the South China tiger, and the Bengal (or Indian) tiger.

Tigers are the biggest cats in the world.
Their powerful jaws and teeth are
designed to crush bones and tear flesh.

Young tigers stay close to their mothers
until they are about two years old.

Although the Siberian, or Amur, tiger's legs are shorter than those of other tiger subspecies, its paws are the largest.

Each subspecies looks a little different from the others. For example, the Siberian tiger lives in the Russian Far East. It has a heavy winter coat to help it survive in snowy surroundings. The Siberian tiger's thick, long fur sets it apart from tigers living in warmer places. While most tigers have black stripes, the Siberian tiger has brown stripes on a pale orange coat. Its underbelly is white to help it blend in with the snow on the ground. Its stripes blend in with bushes and trees.

Siberian tigers are the largest tigers of all. Males can weigh up to 675 pounds (304 kilograms) and are nearly 11 feet (3.3 meters) long. As with all other tiger subspecies, male Siberian tigers are bigger than females. But female Siberians are still big, weighing about 285 pounds (128 kilograms) on average. These tigers have to be large. They live in a colder climate than any other tiger subspecies, so they need a larger body, which can produce more heat. Over thousands of years, they have evolved, or changed, to have shorter legs and tails than other tiger subspecies, making it easier to keep warm.

Scientists who study animals are called zoologists (zoe-OL-uh-jists). They estimate that about 400 Siberian tigers live in the wild today.

Tigers
FUNFACT:

"White" tigers are just a rare color of tiger, not a different animal or subspecies. They are generally only found in zoos.

The tiger spends much of the day resting but is always alert to the sights and sounds of the animals it hunts for food.

Sumatran tigers are the smallest tiger subspecies. Measuring about 8 feet (2.4 meters) from head to tail, male Sumatran tigers may weigh 265 pounds (120 kilograms), which is less than half the weight of their Siberian relatives!

Between 400 and 500 Sumatran tigers live in the wild, mainly in Sumatra's parks and reserves. The island of Sumatra is covered with hot and moist rain forests filled with lush, green plants. It makes a good habitat, or home, for these tigers.

The Sumatran tiger's fur helps it blend in with its surroundings. This is called camouflage (KAM-uh-flaj).

The Sumatran tiger may be the smallest of the five subspecies, but it is still big. Even the smaller females weigh just under 200 pounds (90 kilograms)!

There is very little white in the dark orange coat, except for narrow bands of dirty white on the chest and belly. White would show up too clearly in the lush, green rain forest and make it more difficult for the tiger to travel without being seen. Stripes on the Sumatran tiger are black, and these tigers have more stripes, more closely packed together, than any other subspecies. Their stripes continue down the front legs, something not seen in Siberian tigers. Each tiger has a different pattern of stripes, and researchers sometimes use stripes to identify individual animals within a subspecies.

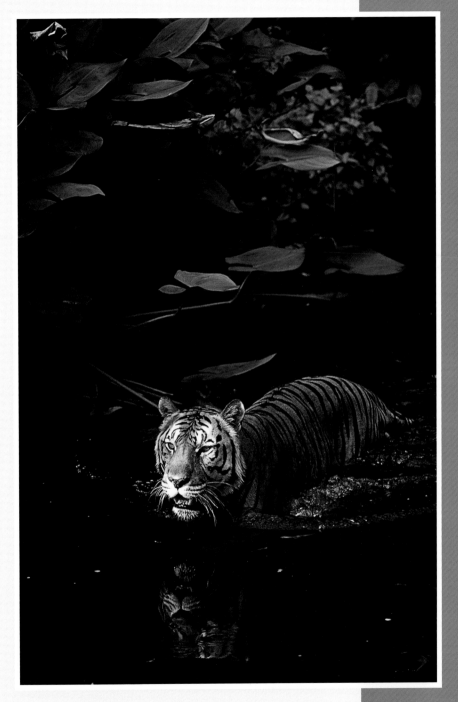

Unlike house cats, tigers spend quite a bit of time in the water—either cooling off, as this Sumatran tiger is doing, or hunting for food.

The Indo-Chinese tiger is found in more countries than any other tiger subspecies. About 1,500 of them are believed to live in the wild. They roam the hills and mountains of China, Myanmar (formerly Burma), Thailand, Cambodia, Laos, Vietnam, and Malaysia.

Indo-Chinese tigers are larger than their Sumatran relatives but still much smaller than Siberian tigers. Their coats are a warm, dark orange with black stripes. Indo-Chinese tigers have fewer stripes, farther apart, than Sumatran tigers but have more stripes and darker coats than their Siberian relatives.

No other tiger subspecies is in greater danger of becoming extinct, or dying out, than the South China tiger. Only 20 or 30 are thought to live in the wild. Male South China tigers are about 8 feet (2.4 meters) long and weigh about 330 pounds (150 kilograms). This tiger's orange coat has shorter, broader, and more openly spaced stripes than does the coat of the Siberian tiger.

Just as humans do, tigers learn by playing. Here, a young
Indo-Chinese tiger is play-fighting with its mother.

The tiger most people know is the Bengal tiger. These tigers live mainly in India, although some are found in Nepal, Bangladesh, Bhutan, and Myanmar. There are more tigers in India than in any other country in the world. Of the estimated 5,000 to 7,000 tigers in the wild, over half are Bengal tigers.

The average male Bengal tiger is about 9½ feet (2.9 meters) long and weighs about 480 pounds (220 kilograms). This tiger's dark orange coat with black stripes is similar to that of the Indo-Chinese tiger. The hair around its face is long, often making a "fringe."

The Bengal tiger's stripes are closer together than those of a South China tiger, and farther apart than those of a Sumatran tiger. Its underbelly fur is bright white, and it has fewer stripes on its front legs than a Sumatran tiger does. Without knowing where a tiger lives, however, even scientists have trouble telling different tiger subspecies apart.

Indo-Chinese tiger

South China tiger

Sumatran tiger

The face of this Bengal, or Indian, tiger is framed by a fringe of fur.

Tigers can live in many different kinds of habitats. While Siberian tigers thrive in snowy pine forests and Sumatran tigers prowl lush rain forests, Bengal tigers often live on dryer lands. Tigers in India live in grassy jungles and in forests with lakes. Indo-Chinese and South China tigers inhabit forests in remote hills or mountains.

Wherever tigers live, they need three important things. First, areas of thick trees and tall grasses are used as cover for hiding from enemies. Second, because tigers are carnivores (KAR-nuh-vorz), or meat eaters, they need lots of prey (PRAY). These are animals to hunt and eat. Third, tigers need a good supply of water to drink.

Tigers
FUNFACT:

According to Chinese tradition, the next "Year of the Tiger" will be in 2010.

The Bengal tiger's habitat often has months of dry weather, so a pond like this one is essential to the animal's survival.

A Sumatran tiger easily hides in the dense growth of its rain forest habitat.

Adult tigers fight over territory, sometimes causing serious injury.

To find the things they need to survive, adult tigers may travel long distances, especially if prey animals are scarce. The area where a tiger lives and roams is called its territory. The size of a tiger's territory varies, depending on the number of prey animals that live there. A female Bengal tiger's territory may be about 10 square miles (26 square kilometers). Male tigers require larger territories, often overlapping those of several females.

Female Siberian tigers may have territories of well over 135 square miles (350 square kilometers)—more than 13 times the size of a female Bengal tiger's territory! Male Siberians range over even more land.

When a male tiger's territory overlaps those of females, the females may become mates for the male. Males often fight among themselves over the best territory and over mates. The losing male must leave the area to find another territory. The winning male stays in the area and mates with nearby females. Females usually spend all of their lives in the same territory. While female lions and their cubs live and hunt in groups known as prides, adult male tigers spend most of their lives alone.

Both males and females regularly travel through their territories, often at night. They may rest during the warm daylight hours in the same spot for several days in a row, but they rarely have a permanent home. A tiger's resting area is often a protected spot in tall grass or other good cover located near water. When a female tiger, or tigress, gives birth, she chooses an even more private spot, such as a cave, where she can hide her babies.

A young female tiger may live close to her mother's territory, but young males usually leave the area, sometimes settling far from their birthplace.

Adult tigers are so big that their only major predators (PRED-uh-torz), or enemies, are other tigers. Female tigers are smaller than males, but they are still very large animals. Female Bengal tigers, for example, weigh between 221 and 353 pounds (99–159 kilograms). That compares to between 419 and 569 pounds (189 and 256 kilograms) for the average male Bengal.

Much of that weight is muscle. A tiger's strong legs help it run in bursts of up to 35 miles (56 kilometers) per hour. They use their tails—3 to 4 feet (about 1 meter) of pure muscle—to help keep their balance while running and turning. Their powerful paws crash down on prey with great force.

Tigers
FUNFACT:

Even though tigers prefer meat, they sometimes eat grass. It's probably to cure an upset stomach!

A tiger's tail is about half as long as its body. While a tiger most often uses its tail to maintain balance while running, it also uses it to communicate with other tigers.

A Bengal tiger's sharp canine teeth are as long as the blade on a pocketknife and just as sharp.

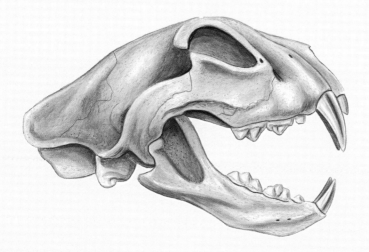

A tiger's large jaws are strong enough to grab and hold prey. Some of their teeth, called canines (KAY-nines), are used to grab and bite prey animals. These teeth are very sharp and are located at the front of the upper and lower jaw. They may measure up to 3 inches (7.5 centimeters) long. If your upper canines were that long, they would reach below your chin! Tigers have a total of 30 teeth, compared to 32 in humans. Like other carnivores, tigers have razor-sharp back teeth called carnassials (kar-NASS-ee-uls). These teeth help tigers rip apart flesh and crush bones.

Tigers don't rely on just their size and strength for survival. Tigers have very good hearing, better than that of humans. Their ears can move to follow the sound of prey animals and predators. Their eyes seem to slant upward, with round black pupils and large yellow-orange irises. Tigers have the good eyesight you would expect from a relative of the house cat. In fact, a tiger's eyesight at night is about six times better than that of humans. Traveling at night is no problem for a tiger, especially when it combines its keen hearing and eyesight with its good sense of smell.

The tiger has an extremely good sense of smell, allowing it
to sniff out its prey and to keep track of other tigers.

A tiger's snout ends with a sensitive orange-pink nose. Bristly whiskers extend from the tiger's cheek, adding to the animal's sense of touch. A tiger often uses its sense of smell to sniff out other tigers in or near its territory. Other tigers leave clues behind them. While traveling, they may stop to spray trees with their urine. They may rub their cheeks against trees or rocks, leaving scent (SENT), or odor, other tigers can smell. Or they may urinate or leave droppings, called scat, on the ground. These signs are ways tigers have of communicating their location, usually to let other male tigers know to stay away.

When a tigress is ready to mate, she marks her territory more often than usual. While marking, she makes a special sound to let any nearby males know that she is ready to mate.

Males may make several kinds of vocalizations (vo-kul-ize-A-shuns), or sounds. They growl, snarl, and even roar, usually to scare off other tigers or animals trying to steal food. Compared to lions, though, tigers don't roar very much. Generally tigers are quiet animals. Researchers believe that tigers, unlike house cats, do not purr when they are happy. This may be caused by differences in the two cats' throat bones.

Tigers
FUNFACT:

Pictures of tigers have appeared on postage stamps in countries around the world, including China, Canada, Sweden, and the United States.

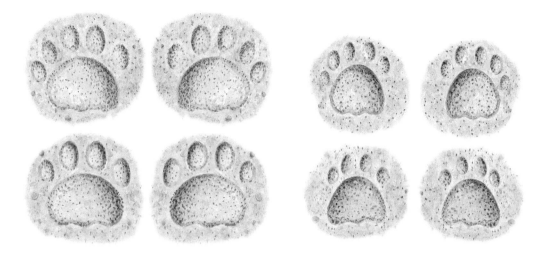

Male pugmarks   Female pugmarks

Zoologists study tiger movements by looking at their paw prints, which are also called pugmarks. Pugmarks can be used to identify different subspecies. Prints from Siberian tigers, for example, are the biggest of any subspecies. Sumatran tigers have the smallest paw prints, averaging about 5 inches (13 cm) in length.

Pugmarks are also sometimes used to identify individual animals. Male tigers have bigger, wider, and more squared pugmarks than females. Some tigers have visible injuries to the five toes on their front feet or the four toes on their rear feet.

Claw marks are not visible in paw prints. Tigers use their sharp claws, which are about 3½ inches (9 centimeters) long, to climb short distances up trees to capture prey or to scratch trees when marking territory. But, like house cats, tigers retract, or pull in, their claws when not tearing or scratching. By studying tracks, researchers learn more about tiger travel and how tigers live.

Just as a house cat sharpens its claws on a carpet-covered "tree," this Bengal tiger claws tree bark. Claw marks set the boundaries for a tiger's territory.

Much of a tiger's time is spent sitting, lying down, and sleeping. Tigers are hard to see when they are at rest in tall grass, amid trees, or among thick bushes. Their stripes break up the outline of their orange coats, helping them blend in with their surroundings. When they stop to rest, tigers often groom themselves. They carefully lick clean their paws, chest, and back using their long, strong tongues. Tigers may then yawn a few times and rest or take a nap, but tigers don't stay in one place for long. As they crisscross their territory, they may take a quick drink in a pond or stream.

Because tigers are mainly active at night, when they do most of their hunting, they are called nocturnal (nok-TURN-ul) animals. If they feel safe, they may sometimes hunt during the daytime.

Whenever they choose to hunt, tigers must have patience. Only about 1 in 20 hunts is successful. Tigers increase their chances of success by watching their prey very carefully.

Tigers usually blend in with their surroundings, but this white tiger stands out wherever it goes. White tigers are a rare color form and not a separate subspecies. Because of their coloring, they generally do not survive long in the wild.

Young tigers, or cubs, often first learn to hunt by observing smaller prey. In India, for example, Bengal cubs begin by hunting langurs. These monkeys are safe from tigers when they stay high in the trees. But when the monkeys come out of the trees to drink at watering holes, cubs are already waiting, hidden in the grasses. When the time is right, the cub pounces, or suddenly jumps out of its hiding place. If it is lucky, the cub will surprise the monkey and make it a meal.

The Bengal tiger's favorite prey animal is the sambar, a type of large deer. Siberian tigers eat the Siberian wapiti, a kind of elk. But tigers don't hunt just one kind of prey. Bengal tigers, for example, also hunt wild boar, wild cattle, monkeys, and peacocks.

Tigers may eat almost any kind of meat if they are hungry enough. From the presence of quills in tiger scat, we know that tigers eat porcupines. Encounters with porcupines—and their long, sharp quills—can cause serious injury to tigers. Tigers also may eat other tigers.

Six-month-old Bengal tiger cubs are about the size of a large dog—
big enough to begin learning to hunt on their own.

Tigers use several different methods when hunting and killing their prey. Often tigers select a daytime resting place close to a source of water. As the day grows warmer, other animals come to the lake or stream. If they are thirsty enough, they take the risk of exposing themselves to a tiger's attack in order to get a drink of cooling water. Some animals wait to drink at night. But tigers are watching and waiting then, too.

When hunting, a tiger may simply remain in one place and wait until its prey has wandered close by. Or it may slowly and silently stalk, or sneak up on, its prey. The soft, cushioning pads on the bottoms of its paws help the tiger move very quietly. Once close enough, the tiger pounces and attacks. When tigers chase their prey, they can leap at least 15 feet (4.5 meters) in one bound.

Tigers
FUNFACT:

Tigers are good swimmers. They cool off in water during hot weather. They also stalk prey in ponds and streams, sometimes swimming many yards, but tigers don't like to get their heads wet. They usually go into the water tail first.

After a long night of hunting, a Bengal tiger still stalks prey along the water's edge.

Tigers may leap, lunge, and pounce many times before they capture prey.
Only five percent of hunts are successful.

Bengal tigers are very successful in hunting their main prey animal, the sambar, by stalking and pouncing. Sambars have an excellent sense of smell, but their eyesight is poor compared to that of the tiger. As long as a tiger can stay out of the wind and keep its scent from getting to the sambar's nose, it has a good chance of capturing its prey. When a sambar does smell a tiger, it bellows. That alarm call tells the whole herd to flee, or run away.

If the tiger catches the sambar before it starts to bellow, it usually kills the animal with its powerful jaws. While a blow from a tiger's paw can stun a smaller prey animal, the sambar is large and fast. It must be stopped in another way. Tigers usually leap upon the sambar and sink their long canine teeth into the animal's neck. Then they quickly swing the body from side to side until the animal stops moving. Sambar and other large prey usually die when the tiger's grip on the neck makes breathing impossible. Tigers sometimes manage to break the necks of smaller prey first.

After the kill, a tiger drags the prey's body, or carcass, into the shelter of tall grass or woods. It wants to be sure that no other animal will find and steal its kill. Tigers may leave the area briefly to find water, but they are very protective of their kills. When possible, a tiger covers the carcass with sticks or branches to hide it from scavenger animals, such as vultures, and other tigers.

When it comes to eating, the tiger is efficient and leaves little to waste. It uses its canine teeth to tear the meat from the bones. A tiger usually feeds on a larger animal starting from the hind end. When the meat is gone, the tiger may use its strong jaws to crush and eat the smaller bones. During times of drought, or a long period of very dry weather, the wet marrow inside the bones provides tigers with an important source of liquid.

This kind of eating is hard work. Tigers generally eat for an hour or so before resting. A tiger continues to eat and sleep near its prey until all the meat is gone, even if it takes several days. In one night, a tiger can eat as much as 50 pounds (23 kilograms) of meat!

If a larger tiger challenges a smaller one over a carcass, the smaller tiger will usually leave, but not without a fight. One or both of them may be seriously injured. Tigers prefer not to feed together, except when a female shares a kill with her cubs.

Tigers
FUNFACT:

Tigers can kill prey animals weighing up to 2,200 pounds (about 1,000 kilograms), many times their own weight.

Tigers do not usually share carcasses with other adults,
but mother tigers share with their cubs.

A mother watches over her young. Cubs face many dangers—illness, starvation, and attack. Scientists believe that of every 100 cubs born, only 50 will survive.

A tigress is ready to mate when she is 3½ to 4 years old. Tigers can mate at any time of the year but are more likely to mate in the cool season. For Bengal tigers, mating usually takes place from November to April. After mating, the male takes no more interest in the female or in raising the family.

Before she gives birth, the female often chooses a cave or other hidden place for her den. The cubs will be almost helpless at birth. She must be sure they will be safe from predators and protected from the weather.

Female tigers are very successful at keeping their babies out of sight. In fact, zoologists have rarely seen cubs younger than three or four months old in the wild. Most of what we know about the early weeks of a tiger's life comes from studies of animals in zoos.

The cubs are born about three months after mating. Tigers generally give birth to litters, or groups, of two to four cubs. Whatever the size of the litter, the number of male and female cubs is usually equal. Soon after birth, the mother licks her babies' fur clean. This licking helps a cub's digestion and blood circulation start working properly. Grooming also keeps the cubs clean so their new scent will not attract predators.

Cubs born in the wild are rarely seen during the first few months of life. A tigress keeps her litter well hidden until the cubs begin to defend themselves.

Newborn tigers weigh about 2 or 3 pounds (about 1 kilogram). Their eyes remain closed for 3 to 14 days after they are born. Even then, they don't see well until they are several weeks old. Cubs nurse, or drink milk, from their mother. Cubs add meat to their diets when they are around six to eight weeks old, but they may continue to nurse until they are about one year old.

Keeping up her strength while nursing and providing meat to cubs is hard work for a mother tiger. She may have to leave her cubs to hunt as often as every other day. Until they are a few months old, the cubs stay close to the protection of the den. If a mother tiger thinks that her den is no longer safe, she moves her cubs to a new site, or location. When her babies are very small, she gently picks them up, one by one, with her teeth and carries them to their new den.

To keep her young cubs safe, a mother may only allow them to leave the den with her at night. Smaller cats, such as leopards, will attack unprotected cubs. Male tigers are another threat. If a male tiger thinks that cubs are not his offspring, he may try to kill them. This is just one more way for a male tiger to protect his territory. A mother tiger warns her cubs of danger by making high, squeaky noises or soft grunts.

Cubs can crawl through thick bushes and grasses before they are about two weeks old. Beginning when they are three or four months old, cubs may be led out of the den to share the mother's kill. They also will play among themselves, pretending to stalk each other like prey and then pouncing.

By the time the cubs are about six months old, they are the size of large dogs. They have learned many things, such as how to find their own mother by following her scent in case they become lost.

Tigers use their tongues for grooming, or keeping clean.

Young cubs often follow their mother and quietly watch her hunt. As they grow older, the cubs begin to stalk and hunt, too. A mother may injure her prey and allow her cubs to finish off the kill. That way, the cubs learn important hunting skills.

By the time they are 1½ years old, the cubs have gotten their permanent teeth. Now they are able to make their own kills. They spend more and more time away from their mother. They explore streams and ponds where prey go for water. They follow trails and paths around their mother's territory, learning the landscape. They play and hunt among themselves.

When they are about two years old, the cubs leave their mother's territory to find a territory of their own. Sometimes two or more cubs from the same litter may travel and live together for a short time after they leave their mother. But soon they begin to live the solitary life of the tiger. Tigers in the wild usually live to be about 10 to 15 years old.

A Siberian tiger plays with her cub in a stream.

All five tiger subspecies are endangered. Only conservation programs can ensure the survival of these fierce and beautiful creatures.

Tigers today live in parts of the world where the human population is growing rapidly. All tiger subspecies are endangered, which means they are in danger of dying out.

Thousands of Siberian, Indo-Chinese, and other tigers have been hunted and killed illegally so their bones could be used in traditional Chinese medicine. For many years in India, Bengal tigers have competed for land with cattle herders. In the mid-1900s, the tiger populations were decreasing rapidly. A program called Project Tiger began to reverse that trend in the 1980s. The program established several parks and reserves where tigers are protected. Bengal tiger populations increased in the late 1980s and 1990s. Siberian tiger habitats in Russia also are being protected with the hope that tiger numbers there will soon increase.

Fortunately, many people are working hard to study and protect the endangered tiger. The more we know about these beautiful and powerful animals, the more likely they will survive for centuries to come.

Internet Sites

You can find out more interesting information about tigers and lots of other wildlife by visiting these web sites.

http://endangered.fws.gov/kids/ — U.S. Fish and Wildlife Service

www.5tigers.org — The Tiger Information Center

www.discovery.com — Discovery Channel Online

www.EnchantedLearning.com — Enchanted Learning

www.kidsgowild.com — Wildlife Conservation Society

www.kidsplanet.org — Defenders of Wildlife

www.nationalgeographic.com/kids — National Geographic Society

www.nwf.org/kids — National Wildlife Federation

www.tnc.org — The Nature Conservancy

www.worldwildlife.org — World Wildlife Fund

Index

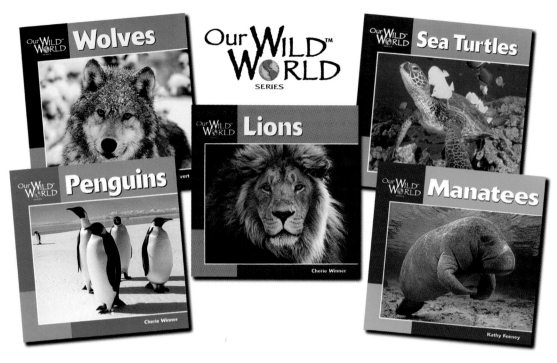

Paperback titles available in the Our Wild World Series:

BISON
ISBN 1-55971-775-0

BLACK BEARS
ISBN 1-55971-742-4

CARIBOU
ISBN 1-55971-812-9

COUGARS
ISBN 1-55971-788-2

DOLPHINS
ISBN 1-55971-776-9

EAGLES
ISBN 1-55971-777-7

LEOPARDS
ISBN 1-55971-796-3

LIONS
ISBN 1-55971-787-4

MANATEES
ISBN 1-55971-778-5

MOOSE
ISBN 1-55971-744-0

PENGUINS
ISBN 1-55971-810-2

SEA TURTLES
ISBN 1-55971-746-7

SHARKS
ISBN 1-55971-779-3

TIGERS
ISBN 1-55971-797-1

WHALES
ISBN 1-55971-780-7

WHITETAIL DEER
ISBN 1-55971-743-2

WOLVES
ISBN 1-55971-748-3

See your nearest bookseller, or order by phone 1-800-328-3895

NorthWord Press
Minnetonka, Minnesota
www.northwordpress.com